The Tattooed Lady in the Garden

Other books by Pattiann Rogers

The Expectations of Light
The Only Holy Window: A Chapbook

Wesleyan Poetry

The Tattooed Lady
in the Garden

Pattiann Rogers

Wesleyan University Press
Middletown, Connecticut

These poems first appeared in the following publications: *Carolina Quarterly, Chowder Review, Domestic Crude, Georgia Review, Iowa Review, Kayak, Poetry, Poetry Northwest, Poetry Now, Prairie Schooner, Southern Review, Virginia Quarterly Review.*
    "The Power of Toads" appeared in *The Pushcart Prize Anthology, IX,* 1984. Several of these poems also appeared in *New American Poets of the 80's* published by Wampeter Press in 1984. "The Art of Becoming" was included in the 1984 edition of *The Anthology of Magazine Verse & Yearbook of American Poetry,* and "The Creation of the Inaudible" was included in the 1985 edition published by The Monitor Book Company, Inc.

Special thanks to the National Endowment for the Arts and the John Simon Guggenheim Foundation for grants that provided opportunities and encouragement during the period when many of these poems were written.

Jacket illustration by William E. Tall, Jr.

All inquiries and permissions requests should be addressed to the Publisher, Wesleyan University Press, 110 Mt. Vernon Street, Middletown, Connecticut 06457.

Distributed by Harper & Row Publishers, Keystone Industrial Park, Scranton, Pennsylvania 18512.

LIBRARY OF CONGRESS CATALOGING IN PUBLICATION DATA
Rogers, Pattiann, 1940–
    The tattooed lady in the garden.
    (Wesleyan poetry)
    I. Title   II. Series
PS3568.0454T36   1986   811'.54   85-7624
ISBN 0-8195-5145-7 (alk. paper)
ISBN 0-8195-6149-5 (pbk. : alk. paper)

Manufactured in the United States of America

First Edition
Wesleyan Poetry

For my mother, Irene C. Keiter Tall, and in memory of my father, William E. Tall, Sr. with gratitude and love, and for John, always

Contents

I

The Pieces of Heaven

No one alone could detail that falling—the immediate
Sharpening and blunting of particle and plane,
The loosening, the congealing of axis
And field, the simultaneous opening and closing
Composing the first hardening of moment when heaven first broke
From wholeness into infinity.

No one alone could follow the falling
Of all those pieces gusting in tattered
Layers of mirage like night rain over a rocky hill,
Pieces cartwheeling like the red-banded leg
Of the locust, rolling like elk antlers dropping
After winter, spiraling slowly like a fossil of squid
Twisting to the bottom of the sea, pieces lying toppled
Like bison knees on a prairie, like trees of fern
In a primeval forest.

And no one could remember the rising
Of all those pieces in that moment, pieces shining
Like cottonwood dust floating wing-side up
Across the bottomland, rising like a woman easily
Lifting to meet her love, like the breasting,
The disappearing surge and scattering crest of fire
Or sea blown against rock, bannered like the quills
Of lionfish in their sway, like the whippling stripe
Of the canebrake rattler under leaves.

Who can envision all of heaven trembling
With the everlasting motion of its own shattering
Into the piece called honor and the piece
Called terror and the piece called death and the piece
Tracing the piece called compassion all the way back
To its source in that initial crimp of potential particle
Becoming the inside and outside called matter and space?

And no one alone can describe entirely
This single piece of heaven partially naming its own falling
Or the guesswork forming the piece
That is heaven's original breaking, the imagined
Piece that is its new and eventual union.

Angel of the Atom

Actual but nonexistent, she is a crease
Of light spinning to a hair-sliver
Of silver in the tip of the needle pointing north.
She is the invisible clutching and releasing
Of the fundamental particles of all summer affirmations,
The length in the flickering wave initiating
The spermatozoa of princes and newts.

Nodding and nodding, she rocks slowly, a real illusion
Buried in the ultimate distinction of the swaying gonad
Of the cottonwood seed. She closes her eyes and creates time
By her steady trembling inside the winter shudder
Of an elm twig filled with eggs.

And she floats above the pond with the silent drift
Of indistinguishable trillions, weaving and flocking,
Rising through the reeds like fog. What a joy
To turn completely once in the sky with dawn, to change,
By that turning, the spread of the sun from coral to gold.

Chanting to herself as she circles in the expanse
Of her disappearing orbits, she is the syllabic movement
Of the cricket's leg, the voweling burr of the bullfrog's
Throat, the still hollow echo of the bottomless cave
Of spring filled with stars. More than herself,
She is both sound and breeze caught in the upper branches
Of the birches constituting the mountain forest she composes.

And when she folds her transparent wings like a soft
Skin of morning around her knees and arms and sleeps,
She dreams of the reality of the vision
Of multiple energy existing inside her dream
Of the nucleus soaring into night.

A measurable body sustaining the immeasurable,
She presses herself continually upward
Through the inner walls of crotch and spine,
Filling breath and vein, hearing the sound of her own name
Spoken by the voice she becomes in the brain.
She meets herself continually as heaven in the eye.
And I know that what I can never perceive is simply
That instant of darkness she imagines she holds tightly forever
Inside the perfect clasp of her shining hands.

Second Witness

The only function of the red-cupped fruit
Hanging from the red stem of the sassafras
Is to reveal the same shiny blue orb of berry
Existing in me.

The only purpose of the row of hemlocks blowing
On the rocky ridge is to give form to the crossed lines
And clicking twigs, the needle-leaf matrix
Of evergreen motion I have always possessed.

Vega and the ring nebula and the dust
Of the Pleiades have made clear by themselves
The constellations inherent to my eyes.

What is it I don't know of myself
From never having seen a crimson chat at its feeding
Or the dunnart carrying its young? It must be imperative
That I watch the entire hardening of the bud
Of the clove, that I witness the flying fish breaking
Into sky through the sun-smooth surface of the sea.

I ask the winter wren nesting in the clogged roots
Of the fallen oak to remember the multitoned song
Of itself in my ears, and I ask the short-snouted
Silver twig weevil to be particular and the fishhook
Cactus to be tenacious. I thank the distinct edges
Of the six-spined spider crab for their peculiarities
And praise the freshwater eel for its graces. I urge
The final entanglement of blade and light to keep
Its secrecy, and I beg the white-tailed kite this afternoon,
For my sake, to be keen-eyed, to soar well, to be quick
To make me known.

Maintaining the Indistinguishable

Sonia and Cecil are surprised to learn
That the large, snow-covered objects dotting
The beach across the lake are not stones
Or pieces of broken ice washed ashore,
But whooper swans, waiting through the storm, drawn-in
And pressed close to the earth, their heads out of sight
Beneath their wings, their bodies gradually
Becoming indistinguishable from the snowdrifts
Building on the beach.

Gordon, sitting by the fire inside, likes to imagine
The white snow slowly covering the white swans, snow so light
Its only recognizable touch is cold, and the invisible
Black spaces caught inside the crystals
Of each white flake. And he likes to imagine the thick
White feathers beneath the snow, feathers so soft
A blind man might miss their touch, and the dark
Spaces caught deep inside the down of each soft barb.
And beneath the feathers, he likes to imagine the swans
So real their most definite touch is the shudder
Of the invisible spaces of light caught inside their black eyes,
Spaces almost indistinguishable from the blind
Crystals caught against the windows looking out
On the white cavity of the storm.

Felicia is excited by this discovery
And has convinced Albert to join her in fashioning
Swans of snow all along the lakefront before the house.
Afterward they will curl up on the shore,
Put their faces under their arms and wait in the falling snow
Until Sonia tells them they are indistinguishable
From the snow-swans they have created on the beach,
Which are indistinguishable from the swanlike drifts
Spanning the snowy shore, which are indistinguishable
From the whooper swans waiting across the dark lake,
Sleeping inside the falling black spaces caught
Inside the touch of white caught inside their eyes.
Felicia and Albert, curled inside the black cavity
Of sleep inside the swans they have invented inside themselves,
Are also able to maintain such spaces.

Gordon is certain that all swanlike figures
Are completely indistinguishable from the white shudder
Of words caught in the act of creating
Their most peculiar distinctions.

The Doctrine

Someone might think there is a tiny human fetus
Alive and curled inside each bristled germ
Of the bottlebrush grass in the field this afternoon.
Someone might imagine those infants inside their clear shells
Deep beyond the plumules of the brown seeds
Of the sow thistle, at the bottom of the frostlike
Blooms of the blackhaw. And someone might picture
Each one perfectly contained, drifting inside a coral
And white light of its own, shining in its nurturing oils,
The rich purple cord buoyant over knees and heels,
Across the buttocks, latched to the belly buried
Inside each white spore of every violet larkspur.

And someone might think those tiny unborn children fill
The sea, tumbling in their soft crystal cases, their thumbs
At their mouths, encompassed by seaweed, sucking
With the filefish and the sargassum crabs, secure
Inside the cave of the cuttlefish, inside the ovaries
Of the dragonet, rising with the spittle of the archerfish;
That they are the first whisper heard on shore
By the boneless tadpole of the spadefoot toad, the first shudder
Felt in the wet paper wings of the darner fly; that they hang
In midair in the colored silk sac of the marbled spider,
Mingling with the claws and fangs, the spinnerets
Of the fetal araneus.

And someone might think they can be seen scattered faraway
Across a black heaven, embryos of breathing light,
That they are the point pulsing in the core of every star
Caught like candles in mantles of glass, that they float
Inside the cells inside the cells of their own eyes,
That they see themselves turning slowly and perfectly
Inside their own hearts, the only center inside the center
Around which they turn in the sky and in the earth
And in the sea, and someone might even *believe*
A thing like that.

The Faulty Realization of the Hoary Puccoon

Felicia's uncle is insane. Completely aware
Of being caught in an unfinished expression of his own,
He believes he is the hoary puccoon. He believes
He grows in grey, nearly stalkless leaves
Among the rocky borders of the grasslands to the north
Which he watches all day from his window.
He has relinquished his fingers and his feet. The soup
Drips from his mouth. He doesn't know his tongue.
He lies, a scatter of blossoms spreading as orange
Corolla with five flaring lobes almost immobile
Under the sky, across the dry, dusty borders
Of his velvet settee.

At dusk he grows violent, fearful
Of his approaching blindness, the gradual advancement
Of his own destruction. At midnight, still staring
From the window in despair, he can see no way at all
To exist.

How can the actual white-haired, five-inch stems
Of the hoary puccoon be expected to bear the weight
Of a witness such as this? Even if they wanted,
The four barely emerging nutlets aiming toward August
Could never be made to accommodate such an expansion.

If he could just decide to leave the field
As the hoary puccoon and enter the realization
In the eyes of the man who watches from the window;
If he could just see himself leaving the field,
Moving as bright orange flowers through the air
Into the bright orange flowers of his retina;
If he could just rise and leave the field
As the branches of narrow articulated leaves and unite
With the identical, sun-flecked leaves inside
His voice, then he might remember once again
What it is he still has to say.

Felicia has been told that it will never do to speak
To the rooted, wind-blown, stalwart, orange-filled
Hoary puccoon of the field.
He knows better than to hear, realizing,
As terminal cluster of tubular flowers,
He has already said everything
He can ever know to say.

Duality

Sonia says a single perfect tree lives inside her,
That the more she tries the more distinctly she can see it,
As if it stood alone on a hill against a light sky,
All the tangled details of its barks and girders and tapering
Twig crosses revealing themselves clearly. She says
She can examine the impetus in the brown, folded nubs
Of its new leaves if she wishes. She says the tree
Is stationary and multitudinous in her chest, untouched
And skeletal, almost like metal, in its network against the sky.

And Sonia told Gordon the tree fills her body
Without pressure, its roots becoming one with her veins
And arteries. She can feel the small limber tips
Of its branches constantly in the palms of her hands.
She can detect, in her breath, the invention of its shifting
Attitude toward changing light. Anyone trained to look
With a scalpel could find its hardwood beginning in her brain.

Sonia says she wills the existence of the tree
By giving it a name, she wills the reality
Of the tree by giving it the location of her own body.
Sonia almost believes that the tree, created by the mind
But united with the body, can give the flesh eternity.

Gordon, laughing, calls it the Tree of Life.

Her Delight

After Psalms 1:2, 3

The tupelo, the blackgum and the poplar,
The overcup oak and the water hickory stand
Along the riverbank being eternal law all day.
They have risen, transforming soil, yielding
To each other, spreading and bending in easy-sun
Contortions, just as their branches decreed they must
During their rising.

Their shadows cast shadow-law this evening
In the long narrow bars of steady black they make
Over the river, being the permanent mathematical
Matrixes they invent relative to the height
Of their ascending trunks.

And the law taking in the soft moisture
Of slow, pervading rivers underground
Is called root. And the root consistently sorting
Ion and mineral by the describable properties
Of its gated skin is called law.

The plum-shaped fruit of the tupelo
Is the rule defining the conformity
To which it shapes itself. The orange berry
Of the possumhaw creates the sugary orange law

Of the sun by which it makes its reality.
Every flattened pit and dark blue drupe and paper-skin
Seed obeys perfectly the commandment it fashions
By becoming itself.

The trees only write the eternal law
Of whatever they have written—the accomplishment
Of the blackgum ordaining autumn red
In the simultaneous commandment of its scarlet leaves;
The accomplishment of the hickory branching
Its leaf in naked, thin-veined everlasting statutes
Of yellow across the sky.

And the woman standing this evening beneath the river trees,
Watching them rise by fissured bark, by husked and hardened
Fruit held high above the water, watching the long bodies
Of their shadows lying unmoved across the current,
She is the easy law that states she must become,
In the hazy, leaf-encroached columns of the evening sun,
Her meditation in this delight.

Raising the Eyes That High

It always happens, looking up to the tops
Of the sycamores still white and yellow with sunlight
Above the dark river bottom, or bending back to see
The wind, heard first as a caravan of paper horses
In the upper branches of the pines, or following
The flurried lightning bug to where it disappears
Above the parsley haw then catches on again
Even higher, raising the eyes that high,
The body begins to feel again something of significance.

Maybe it's the result of some predisposition
We've inherited from the trees, something in the genes
Promoting a belief in the importance of ascension
Or reaffirming the 70-million-year-old conviction
That stretching one leaf higher might be enough
To finally discover the sky. There's a feeling
In the body of a conviction like that.

Maybe the act of tilting the head backward
To search the sky for Mizar or Draco
Merely flexes the spinal cord at the neck,
Thus doubling the strength of every impulse
Passing there, or maybe sight is actually deepened
When blood flows backward from the eyes,
Or maybe more oxygen, helped by gravity
To the frontal lobe, expands the normal boundaries
Of the perceived heavens.

It might be something as simple as that.
But it's certain, watching the pale-pearl angle
Of the early-evening moon, or following the five
Black cowbirds reel across the greying clouds,
Or tracing the easy drift of a cottonwood seed
Slowly rising directly overhead, it's certain,
There's bound to be something new again of power
Astir in the body.

Love Song

It's all right, together with me tonight,
How your whole body trembles exactly like the locust
Establishing its dry-cymbal quivering
Even in the farthest branch-tip leaves
Of the tree in which it screams.

Lying next to me, it's all right how similar
You become to the red deer in its agitated pacing
On the open plains by the sea, in its sidling
Haunch against haunch, in the final mastery
Of its mounting.

And it's all right, in those moments,
How you possess the same single-minded madness
Of the opened wood poppy circling and circling,
The same wild strength of its golden eye.

It's true. You're no better
Than the determined boar snorgling and rooting,
No better than the ridiculous, ruffled drumming
Of the prairie chicken, no better
Than the explosion of the milkweed pod
Spilling the white furl of the moon deep
In the midnight field. You're completely
Indistinguishable from the enraged sand myrtle
Absurd in its scarlet spread on the rocky bluffs.

But it's all right. Don't you know
This is precisely what I seek, mad myself
To envelope every last drupe and pearl-dropped ovule,
Every nip and cry and needle-fine boring, every drooping,
Spore-rich tassle of oak flower, all the whistling,
Wing-beating, heavy-tipped matings of an entire prairie
Of grasses, every wafted, moaning seed hook
You can possibly manage to bring to me,
That this is exactly what I contrive to take into my arms
With you, again and again.

The Hummingbird: A Seduction

If I were a female hummingbird perched still
And quiet on an upper myrtle branch
In the spring afternoon and if you were a male
Alone in the whole heavens before me, having parted
Yourself, for me, from cedar top and honeysuckle stem
And earth down, your body hovering in midair
Far away from jewelweed, thistle and bee balm;

And if I watched how you fell, plummeting before me,
And how you rose again and fell, with such mastery
That I believed for a moment *you* were the sky
And the red-marked bird diving inside your circumference
Was just the physical revelation of the light's
Most perfect desire;

And if I saw your sweeping and sucking
Performance of swirling egg and semen in the air,
The weaving, twisting vision of red petal
And nectar and soaring rump, the rush of your wing
In its grand confusion of arcing and splitting
Created completely out of nothing just for me,

Then when you came down to me, I would call you
My own spinning bloom of ruby sage, my funneling
Storm of sunlit sperm and pollen, my only breathless
Piece of scarlet sky, and I would bless the base
Of each of your feathers and touch the tine
Of string muscles binding your wings and taste
The odor of your glistening oils and hunt
The honey in your crimson flare
And I would take you and take you and take you
Deep into any kind of nest you ever wanted.

The Power of Toads

The oak toad and the red-spotted toad love their love
In a spring rain, calling and calling, breeding
Through a stormy evening clasped atop their mates.
Who wouldn't sing—anticipating the belly pressed hard
Against a female's spine in the steady rain
Below writhing skies, the safe moist jelly effluence
Of a final exaltation?

There might be some toads who actually believe
That the loin-shaking thunder of the banks, the evening
Filled with damp, the warm softening mud and rising
Riverlets are the facts of their own persistent
Performance. Maybe they think that when they sing
They sing more than songs, creating rain and mist
By their voices, initiating the union of water and dusk,
Females materializing on the banks shaped perfectly
By their calls.

And some toads may be convinced they have forced
The heavens to twist and moan by the continual expansion
Of their lung sacs pushing against the dusk.
And some might believe the splitting light,
The soaring grey they see above them are nothing
But a vision of the longing in their groins,
A fertile spring heaven caught in its entirety
At the pit of the gut.

And they might be right.
Who knows whether these broken heavens
Could exist tonight separate from trills and toad ringings?
Maybe the particles of this rain descending on the pond
Are nothing but the visual manifestation of whistles
And cascading love clicks in the shore grasses.
Raindrops-finding-earth and coitus could very well
Be known here as one.

We could investigate the causal relationship
Between rainstorm and love-by-pondside if we wished.
We could lie down in the grasses by the water's edge
And watch to see exactly how the heavens were moved,
Thinking hard of thunder, imagining all the courses
That slow, clean waters might take across our bodies,
Believing completely in the rolling and pressing power
Of heavens and thighs. And in the end we might be glad,
Even if all we discovered for certain was the slick, sweet
Promise of good love beneath dark sides inside warm rains.

Betrayal: The Reflection of the Cattail

The black lines of the cattail reeds sway in grace
Before the purple sky. On the stalk above the thick
Brown fruits of the velvet female, I can see the shriveled
Spike of the expended male making slow and crooked
Slices through the early stars.

A single long leaf bends and bows above the lake,
Its narrow tip barely tracing the surface of the water
With the breeze. It moves, making random trails exactly
Like an unfaithful lover makes, tracing with her finger
The features of her only love.

The single arch of a cattail leaf can rest lightly
Like an arm across the glowing belly of a softly falling sun,
And it can bend over the clear water of the lake,
Steady and gentle and graceful as a faithful lover
Bent above the face of his only love.

The slender grasses of the cattail twist now
And turn in a sudden breeze against the purple sky
Like lovers locking their legs at the ankles, like lovers
Turning their thighs once in a sudden locking,
Like lovers opening once to unlock and expose
The sudden gleaming surface of a dark red sun.

In the earth the cattail spreads
And widens its roots and the bases of its reeds.
It presses down and holds on hard as if it believed
The shore was its only faithful lover.
And when the loon cries and when the king rail calls,
The tangled reeds of the cattail stiffen imperceptibly
And move their shining edges among the stars
As if they screamed themselves. And when the loon rises
And when the king rail soars, the reeds shudder
Like tangled lovers feeling the slicing edges
Of a million stars escaping from their bodies to the sky.

The cattail knows how to bear the staunchest grace
Beside the lake, just as if it didn't realize
It was being carried, along with us, across the vast
Deceptive light of forgiveness this evening, through darkness
Into darkness.

At the Break of Spring

Caddisfly larvae, living in clear-water
Streams, construct tiny protective cases
Around themselves with bits of bark,
Grass and pieces of pink gravel in mosaics.

Little temples, Felicia calls them.

Albert loves temples and knows a man who lives
Beside one, the northern wall of his cottage
Being the temple itself. He can imitate perfectly
The running of twelve-tone bells announcing birth or death.

Gordon wants to study the pattern of clear
Running water covering caddisfly larvae in sunlight
And compare it to the pattern of running bells announcing
Death in the clear morning as seen from below.

Felicia thinks caddisfly larvae can forgive any sin
Because they live inside temples underwater
Continually in a state of baptism.

Christ called the body a temple.

Cecil loves bodies and thinks Sonia's is a mosaic,
Dark and unseen, lit as if by light underwater.
To completely cover Sonia himself
Is a baptism of sin Cecil is afraid to perform.

Felicia likes to believe the morning sky
Is a temple immersed in light and, by running
Across the open lawn to the arbor house, she herself might
Become the twelve-tone sounding of its multiple bells.

Sonia, walking beside the stream after dark, thinks
Any temple continually immersed in the light
Of its own birth and death has earned the right to call sin
A baptism of performance, clearly forgivable.

The Possible Salvation of Continuous Motion

Adapted from a love letter
written by E. Lotter (1872–1930)

If we could be taken alone together in a driverless
Sleigh pulled by horses with blinders over endless
Uninhabited acres of snow; if the particles
Of our transgression could be left behind us
Scattered across the woodlands and frozen lakes
Like pieces of light scattered over the flashing snow;

If the initiation and accomplishment of our act
In that sleigh could be separated by miles
Of forest—the careful parting begun
Under the ice-covered cedars, the widening and entering
Accomplished in swirls of frost racing along the hills,
The removal and revelation coming beside the seesaw shifting
Of grassheads rustling in the snowy ditches; all the elements
Of our interaction left in a thousand different places—
Thigh against thigh with the drowsy owlets in the trees
Overhead, your face caught for an instant above mine
In one eye of the snow hare;

If the horses could go fast enough across the ice
So that no one would ever be able to say, "Sin
Was committed *here*," our sin being as diffuse
As broken bells sounding in molecules of ringing
Clear across the countryside;

And under the blanket beside you in the sleigh
If I could watch the night above the flying heads
Of the horses, if I could see our love exploded
Like stars cast in a black sky over the glassy plains
So that nothing, not even the mind of an angel,
Could ever reassemble that deed;

Well, I would go with you right now,
Dearest, immediately, while the horses
Are still biting and strapping in their reins.

The Delight of Being Lost

There are times when one might wish to be nothing
But the plain crease and budded nipple
Of a breast, nothing but the manner in the lay
Of an arm across a pillow or the pressure of hips
And shoulders on a sheet. Sometimes there is a desire
To draw down into the dull turn of the inner knee, dumb
And isolated from the cognizant details of any summer night,
To be chin and crotch solely as the unrecorded, passing
Moments of themselves, to have no name or place but breath.

If wished enough, it might be possible to sink away completely,
To leave the persistent presence of pine trees
Brushing against the eaves, loons circling the lake,
Making an issue of direction; to sink away, remaining
Awake inside the oblivion deep within a naked thigh,
To open the eyes inside the blindness of a wrist, hearing
Nothing but the deafness in the curve of the neck.

It would seem a perfect joy to me tonight
To lie still in this darkness, to deny everything
But the rise in the line of ankle or spine, ignoring
The angles of walls establishing definable spaces,
Ignoring the clear, moon-shadow signals of specific
Circumstance, to recognize no reality but the universal
Anonymity of a particular body which might then be stroked
And kissed and fondled and worshipped without ever knowing
Or caring to ask by whom or where or how it was given
Such pleasure.

An Experiment of Faith

Gordon thinks doubt is the hallmark of our species
Since it brings about inquiry, faith, bravery
And the desire for verification.

Watching the candelabra at dinner, Felicia asked
If flame itself ever had a shadow.

Cecil doubts that flame casts a shadow,
But Sonia will attempt to verify his position
By an experiment to be conducted with three candles
And a torch in the white parlor after dark.
She has named the event, "An Enquiry into the Doubtful
Properties of the Shadow of Light."

Albert is not brave enough to doubt
That his finger held above the flame
Will eventually show a shadow of pain.

Gordon finds it possible to doubt the existence
Of the snow-covered forest just outside the east window
But possesses enough faith to say with certainty
It is the moon again tonight that makes the shadow
Of the branch across the silk drapes.

Though doubting that he will be brave enough
To touch Sonia's breast in the dark tonight
And possibly create thereby a shadow of light,
Cecil allows himself to daydream a verification
Of his faith in its silky warm existence.

Gordon asked Albert to verify the bravery
Of his attempt to prove that absolute faith
Is a prerequisite to doubt, since the existence
Of doubt itself can never be doubted.

A Daydream of Light

We could sit together in the courtyard
Before the fountain during the next full moon.
We could sit on the stone bench facing west,
Our backs to the moon, and watch our shadows
Lying side by side on the white walk. We could spread
Our legs to the metallic light and see the confusion
In our hands bound up together with darkness and the moon.
We could talk, not of light, but of the facets of light
Manifesting themselves impulsively in the falling water,
The moon broken and re-created instantaneously over and over.

Or we could sit facing the moon to the east,
Taking it between us as something hard and sure
Held in common, discussing the origins of rocks
Shining in the sky, altering everything exposed below.
What should I imagine then, recognizing its light
On your face, tasting its light on your forehead, touching
Its light in your hair?

Or we could sit on the bench to the north,
Buried by the overhanging sycamore,
The moon showing sideways from the left.
We could wonder if light was the first surface
Imprinted with fact or if black was the first
Underlying background necessary for illumination.
We could wonder if the tiny weightless blackbirds
Hovering over our bodies were leaf shadows

Or merely random blankness lying between splashes fallen
From the moon. We could wonder how the dark shadow
From a passing cloud could be the lightest
Indication across our eyes of our recognition of the moon.

Or we could lie down together where there are no shadows at all,
In the open clearing of the courtyard, the moon
At its apex directly overhead, or lie down together
Where there are no shadows at all, in the total blackness
Of the alcove facing north. We could wonder, at the end,
What can happen to light, what can happen to darkness,
When there is no space for either left between us.

We must ask if this daydream is light broken
And re-created instantaneously or simply an impulsive
Shadow passing across the light in our eyes,
Finding no space left for its realization.

II

The Definition of Time

In the same moment
That Kioka's great-great-grandfather died,
11,000 particles of frost dissolved into dew
On the blades of the woodrush,
And three water lily leaf beetles paused
Anticipating light making movements
Of their bodies in the weeds.

And in that same moment an earthworm
Swallowed a single red spore down its slimest
Vein, and the chimney crayfish shoveled a whisker farther
Through slick pond-bottom silt, and one slow
Slice of aster separated its purple segment
From the bud.

Simultaneously the mossy granite along the ridge shifted
Two grains on its five-mile fault, and the hooves
Of ewe and pony, damp in the low-field fog,
Shook with that shift. The early hawk on the post
Blinked a drop of mist from its eye, and the black tern
With a cry flew straight up remembering the marsh
By scent alone over the sandy hills.

And in that instant the field, carried
Without consent through the dark, held
Its sedges steady for the first turn
Into the full orange sun, and each tense sliver
Of pine on the mountains far to the east
Shone hot already in a white noon,
And in the dark night-sea far behind the field and forest,
The head of a single shark sperm pierced
An ovum and became blood.

The twelfth ring of the tallest redwood
Hardened its circle, and the first lick of the hatching
Goatweed butterfly was made tongue. And Kioka
And his ancestors call the infinite and continuous
Record they make of this moment "The Book
Of the Beginning and the Chronicle of the End."

The Possible Suffering of a God during Creation

It might be continuous—the despair he experiences
Over the imperfection of the unfinished, the weaving
Body of the imprisoned moonfish, for instance,
Whose invisible arms in the mid-waters of the deep sea
Are not yet free, or the velvet-blue vervain
Whose grainy tongue will not move to speak, or the ear
Of the spitting spider still oblivious to sound.

It might be pervasive—the anguish he feels
Over the falling away of everything that the duration
Of the creation must, of necessity, demand, maybe feeling
The break of each and every russet-headed grass
Collapsing under winter ice or feeling the split
Of each dried and brittle yellow wing of the sycamore
As it falls from the branch. Maybe he winces
At each particle-by-particle disintegration of the limestone
Ledge into the crevasse and the resulting compulsion
Of the crevasse to rise grain by grain, obliterating itself.

And maybe he suffers from the suffering
Inherent to the transitory, feeling grief himself
For the grief of shattered beaches, disembodied bones
And claws, twisted squid, piles of ripped and tangled,
Uprooted turtles and rock crabs and Jonah crabs,
Sand bugs, seaweed and kelp.

How can he stand to comprehend the hard, pitiful
Unrelenting cycles of coitus, ovipositors, sperm and zygotes,
The repeated unions and dissolutions over and over,
The constant tenacious burying and covering and hiding
And nesting, the furious nurturing of eggs, the bright
Breaking-forth and the inevitable cold blowing-away?
Think of the million million dried stems of decaying
Dragonflies, the thousand thousand leathery cavities
Of old toads, the mounds of cows' teeth, the tufts
Of torn fur, the contorted eyes, the broken feet, the rank
Bloated odors, the fecund brown-haired mildews
That are the residue of his process. How can he tolerate knowing
There is nothing else here on earth as bright and salty
As blood spilled in the open?

Maybe he wakes periodically at night,
Wiping away the tears he doesn't know
He has cried in his sleep, not having had time yet to tell
Himself precisely how it is he must mourn, not having had time yet
To elicit from his creation its invention
Of his own solace.

The Possible Advantages of the Expendable Multitudes

There could be a quirk in the conception of time.
For instance, the brief slide of a single herring
In the sights of an ocean bird might be measured,
At the last moment, in a slow motion of milliseconds,
Each fin spread like a fan of transparent bones
Breaking gradually through the green sea, a long
And complete absorption in that one final movement
Of body and wave together. It could be lengthened
To last a lifetime.

Or maybe there is a strange particulate vision
Only possible in a colony of microscopic copepod
Swaying in and out of the sand eel's range, swallowed
Simultaneously by the thousands. Who knows
What the unseen see? There might be a sense
Of broadcast, a fulfillment of scattering felt
Among the barnacle larva, never achieved
By the predatory shag at the top of the chain.
And the meadow vole crouched immediately below
The barred owl must experience a sudden and unusual
Hard hold on the potential.

Death coming in numbers among the small and uncountable
Might be altered in its aspects. An invaded nest
Of tadpoles might perceive itself as an array of points
Lit briefly in a sparkling pattern of extinction
Along the shore. An endless variety of split-second
Scenes might be caught and held visible in the separate eyes
Of each sea turtle penned on the beach. Death,
Functioning in a thousand specific places at once,
Always completing the magnitude of its obligations,
Has never been properly recognized for its ingenuity.

We must consider the possibility
That from the viewpoint of a cluster of flagellates
We might simply appear to be possessed
By an awkward notion of longevity, a peculiar bias
For dying alone.

The Verification of Vulnerability: Bog Turtle

Guarded by horned beak and nails, surrounded
By mahogany carapace molded in tiles
Like beveled wood, hidden within the hingeless
Plastron, beneath twelve, yellow-splotched
Black scutes, buried below the inner lungs
And breast, harbored in the far reaches
Of the living heart, there it exists,
As it must, that particle of vulnerability,
As definite in its place as if it were a brief glint
Of steel, buried inside the body of the bog turtle.

And it is carried in that body daily, like a pinpoint
Of diamond in a dark pouch, through marshy fields
And sunlit seepages, and it is borne in that body,
Like a crystal of salt-light locked in a case
Of night, borne through snail-ridden reeds and pungent
Cow pastures in spring. It is cushioned and bound
By folds of velvet, by flesh and the muscle
Of dreams, during sleep on a weedy tussock all afternoon.
It is divided and bequeathed again in June, protected
By thick sap, by yolk meal and forage inside its egg
Encompassed by the walls of shell and nest.

Maybe I can imagine the sole intention present
In the steady movement of turtle breath filled
With the odor of worms this morning, stirring
Clover moisture at the roots. Maybe I can understand
How the body has taken form solely
Around the possibility of its own death,
How the entire body of the bog turtle
Cherishes and maintains and verifies the existence
Of its own crucial point of vulnerability exactly
As if that point were the only distinct,
Dimensionless instant of eternity ever realized.
And maybe I can guess what it is we own,
If, in fact, it is true: the proof of possession
Is the possibility of loss.

The Limitations of Death

No form of its own at all, less than a wraith,
It is bound forever to the living, totally
Dependent on viable bone, on the breath
Of the oxpecker and the buffalo, on the sustaining
Will of black-billed cuckoo and threaded bittium,
On the success of potential rooting in rhubarb
And bluebonnet seed, for its future.

Nonexistent without the continuous rise
Of bittersweet sapling and loblolly bay, lost,
Doomed, doomed without the prevailing heart
Of the basswood, the heart of the holding madtom,
The heartfelt knot of the chicory, it has no place at all
Except the upward thrust of the aphid, the spreading lips
Of the hawthorn bloom.

So obviously dependent on the continual well-being
Of the living, death must always admit, for the sake
Of its own reality, must always testify to the enduring
Glory of its victims and even in the performance
Of its only act, must continue to praise the proceeding
Diligence of the nursery web spider, the pure structure
Of the muskrat's cave, the focus of the cleaner shrimp
Nibbling carefully at the flank of the angelfish
Far below the sea and the angelfish and the shining
Flank itself, for the predominating ascendancy
They consistently maintain.

Justification of the Horned Lizard

I don't know why the horned lizard wants to live.
It's so ugly—short prickly horns and scowling
Eyes, lipless smile forced forever by bone,
Hideous scaly hollow where its nose should be.

I don't know what the horned lizard has to live for,
Skittering over the sun-irritated sand, scraping
The hot dusty brambles. It never sees anything but gravel
And grit, thorns and stickery insects, the towering
Creosote bush, the ocotillo and its whiplike
Branches, the severe edges of the Spanish dagger.
Even shade is either barren rock or barb.

The horned lizard will never know
A lush thing in its life. It will never see the flower
Of the water-filled lobelia bent over a clear
Shallow creek. It will never know moss floating
In waves in the current by the bank or the blue-blown
Fronds of the water clover. It will never have a smooth
Glistening belly of white like the bullfrog or a dew-heavy
Trill like the mating toad. It will never slip easily
Through mud like the skink or squat in the dank humus
At the bottom of a decaying forest in daytime.
It will never be free of dust. The only drink it will ever know
Is in the body of a bug.

And the horned lizard possesses nothing noble—
Embarrassing tail, warty hide covered with sharp dirty
Scales. No touch to its body, even from its own kind,
Could ever be delicate or caressing.

I don't know why the horned lizard wants to live.
Yet threatened, it burrows frantically into the sand
With a surprisingly determined fury of forehead, limbs
And ribs. Pursued, it even fights for itself, almost rising up,
Posturing on its bowed legs, propelling blood out of its eyes
In tight straight streams shot directly at the source
Of its possible extinction. It fights for itself,
Almost rising up, as if the performance of that act,
The posture, the propulsion of the blood itself,
Were justification enough and the only reason needed.

Eulogy for a Hermit Crab

You were consistently brave
On these surf-drenched rocks, in and out of their salty
Slough holes around which the entire expanse
Of the glinting grey sea and the single spotlight
Of the sun went spinning and spinning and spinning
In a tangle of blinding spume and spray
And pistol-shot collisions your whole life long.
You stayed. Even with the wet icy wind of the moon
Circling your silver case night after night after night
You were here.

And by the gritty orange curve of your claws,
By the soft, wormlike grip
Of your hinter body, by the unrelieved wonder
Of your black-pea eyes, by the mystified swing
And swing and swing of your touching antennae,
You maintained your name meticulously, you kept
Your name intact exactly, day after day after day.
No one could say you were less than perfect
In the hermitage of your crabness.

Now, beside the racing, incomprehensible racket
Of the sea stretching its great girth forever
Back and forth between this direction and another,
Please let the words of this proper praise I speak
Become the identical and proper sound
Of my mourning.

Trinity

I wish something slow and gentle and good
Would happen to me, a patient and prolonged
Kind of happiness coming in the same way evening
Comes to a wide-branched sycamore standing
In an empty field; each branch, not succumbing,
Not taken, but feeling its entire existence
A willing revolution of cells; even asleep,
Feeling a decision of gold spreading
Over its ragged bark and motionless knots of seed,
Over every naked, vulnerable juncture; each leaf
Becoming a lavender shell, a stem-deep line
Of violet turning slowly and carefully to possess exactly
The pale and patient color of the sky coming.

I wish something that slow and that patient
Would come to me, maybe like the happiness
Growing when the lover's hand, easy on the thigh
Or easy on the breast, moves like late light moves
Over the branches of a sycamore, causing
A slow revolution of decision in the body;
Even asleep, feeling the spread of hazy coral
And ivory-grey rising through the legs and spine
To alter the belief behind the eyes; feeling the slow
Turn of wave after wave of acquiescence moving
From the inner throat to the radiance of a gold belly
To a bone center of purple; an easy, slow-turning
Happiness of possession like that, prolonged.

I wish something that gentle and that careful
And that patient would come to me. Death
Might be that way if one knew how to wait for it,
If death came easily and slowly,
If death were good.

The Art of Becoming

The morning, passing through narrowing and widening
Parabolas of orange and spotted sunlight on the lawn,
Moving in shifting gold-grey shawls of silk lying low,
Thinning and rising through stalks of steeplebush
And bedstraw, through the first start of the first finch
Streaking past the vacancy in the sky where the last
White stone of star was last seen, can only be defined
In the constant change of itself.

The particular leaf, pushing its several green molecules
Outward to a hard edge of photosynthesis, microscopic
In its building and bumping continuously
From one moment to the next, only becomes magnolia
In this prolonged act of its dying.

Realization itself is the changing destruction
And process of cells failing and rising constantly
In their creation of thought. If every white glint
On the surface of the holly, every clenching hair
In the amber center of spirea, every sleight of insect
Wing and cactus spire, the creviced tricks
Of fern segment and sunfish blade were halted right now,
In this moment, one instant caught perfectly and lasting forever,
Then "now" would be the only and final statement of this work.

Immortality must only exist in the sound
Of these words recognizing, through the circling and faltering
Of oak peaks, through the knot of midnight tightening
And loosening, through star streams inventing destination
By the fact of their direction, in the sound of these words
Recognizing their need to pray over and over and over
For the continuing procedure of their own decay.

The God of Ornithology

Observed feathers are his pride—the iridescent purple
And blue-grey gloss, the perfect sheen of barb and shaft
Upon vane and hook, the scarlet-gold cacophony.

The snatching and jerking of moss
And rootlets, seaweed and fishbones,
The binding and stitching of straw and tendrils,
The knotting of cobwebs, the twig-tucking and plotting
Of mud, the quick-needled winding and twisting
Of plant down, bark strips and snake skins
Are the supposed mechanisms of his contemplations.

He is the expanded listing of perching birds,
Seed birds, carrion birds and shore birds,
The naming of stall and slot, major pectoral
And minor pectoral. He remembers by the delineation
Of the bones of the Ichthyornis and the Hesperornis.
He feels his own skeleton by the detailed classification
Of bee eaters and goatsuckers, mousebirds, swifts,
Rollers and their allies. The identification of the eye orbit
Of the thrush establishes the field of vision
By which he is able to perceive his own image.

And when the bank swallows are seen soaring upward
He opens his arms wide. And when the pied-billed grebe
Is acknowledged gliding along the surface of the lake,

He breathes deeply. By the recognized spread
Of each pale grey primary feather of the harrier's wing
He achieves dexterity.

Understand how the identification of the rattle
Of the wren is his listening, how the noted tremulo
Of the dove is his acuity, how the recognized shrieks
And quocks and stutterings and trills, the prolonged whistles
Of the grackles provide the means he needs to invent
The compassion that is essential to their survival.

The consideration of the movement of space
Within the scattering of blackbirds molding the sky
Above the field, the consideration of the body
Of the gull forming the ocean fog through which it flies,
The consideration of the gannets constituting the reality
Of the cliff on which they nest, the consideration
Of the fan-shaped descent of every bird verifying
The exact point at which the earth begins, all become
The crisscrossing pattern of his identity maintained
As the only possible medium in which these activities may occur.

Remember how he waits, as if he were settling in the dark
Evening rocks beside the sea, as if he were brooding
Among the tall marsh grasses, as if he were quiet
In the tops of the black jungle trees. Remember how he waits,
Dependent for his creation on the continued discovery
Of every physical manifestation he nurtures.

The Creation of the Inaudible

Maybe no one can distinguish which voice
Is god's voice sounding in a summer dusk
Because he calls with the same rising frequency,
The same rasp and rattling rustle the cicadas use
As they cling to the high leaves in the glowing
Dust of the oaks.

His exclamations might blend so precisely with the final
Crises of the swallows settling before dark
That no one will ever be able to say with certainty,
"That last long cry winging over the rooftop
Came from god."

Breathy and low, the vibrations of his nightly
Incantations could easily be masked by the scarcely
Audible hush of the lakeline dealing with the rocky shore,
And when a thousand dry sheaths of rushes and thistles
Stiffen and shiver in an autumn wind, anyone can imagine
How quickly and irretrievably his whisper might be lost.

Someone faraway must be saying right now:
The only unique sound of his being
Is the spoken postulation of his unheard presence.

For even if he found the perfect chant this morning
And even if he played the perfect strings to accompany it,
Still, no one could be expected to know,
Because the blind click beetle flipping in midair,
And the slider turtle easing through the black iris bog,
And two savannah pines shedding dawn in staccato pieces
Of falling sun are already engaged in performing
The very same arrangement themselves.

Transformation

When the honeysuckle vine blooming beside the barn
First became the white and yellow tangle of her eye,
And the mouse snake passing beneath the dry grasses
Became the long steady hush of her ear, and the spring hill
Was transformed into the rise of her climbing
Bare feet in April;

When the afternoon between the canyon walls
Became the echoing shout of her voice, and the line
Of orange-stone sun, appearing through a crevice
Of granite, shone as the exact hour of her solstice;
When the cold January wind turned to the flesh
Of her stinging fingertips, and the birds flying
Over the rice beds became the seven crows of her count;

When the dawning sun was the beginning rim
Of light showing over the eastern edge of her sight,
And the earth became, for the only time in its history,
The place of her shadow, and the possibilities
Lying faraway between the stars were suddenly
The unwitnessed boundaries of her heart . . .

Felicia was born.

Filling-in Spaces

Watching through the east window this afternoon
Sonia knows there are no empty spaces left
Inside that winter frame. All the lines
Of the field have been filled perfectly with pieces
Of fitted snow, and the field allows no room behind it
As it leans tightly against the crowded blue cedars
On the hillsides. The stream gully has risen slowly
Out of itself, through its own vacancy, becoming one
And identical with field-white.

And in the only spot where a black branch of crooked
Garden ash might exist drawing across the blue hills
And heaven, a bare branch of crooked garden ash exists.
And in the only seams where sky might press
Between blades of icy pine, the sky has penetrated
In needles of grey. Any fallen oak leaf frozen in ice
Can only force the curved edge of its icy hollow
Into the evening by finding the place where evening
Has already discovered its own curl of hollow cold.

Sonia is confident that all spaces are filled
This afternoon, that there is no room left in the window
For anything else, until she sees Albert moving
Across the white field far away, a small but definite
Crack coming between heaven and snow, until she watches
His approaching body as it widens and enlarges
The vacant space it creates by itself in the dusk,

Until she recognizes the real emptiness of his open arms
As he runs toward the window, kicking up spirals of snow
That strike the glass void existing right before Sonia's vision
Just barely beginning now to be filled.

Exposing the Future with Conviction

Grunion have convictions. Coming up out of the sea
Without a doubt, they clear the moon's surface of wave
And salt water completely. They are scarcely able to breathe
In that unhindered light. Even in their silver
Strait jackets they have believed from the beginning
In this particular tide, this particular black beach.
They have seen, before it ever occurred, the glycerin
Eye burning on dry land. How else could they come
With so much certainty?

Think of one egg left behind, buried like a drop
Of oil in the dark sand. Even before the eye in that egg
Is a black dot, even before the heart is a red grain
Sunk in its tiny bubble, every detail of the first high tide
Of next summer and the summer beyond that
Is waiting, caught and held tight inside. Imagine
The whole heaven of the full moon a year from now,
And the black wind over the sea-to-come and the salt air
Cupped in the conch-not-yet-crystallized,
All held in their entireties inside that jelly shell.

What if there were an instrument small enough to locate
And expose all the elements of the future spawnings
Contained in a single grunion gene?
Then from here we could watch next year's moon dripping clear,

Changing its white focus, and we could examine
The sea birds not yet born waiting on the bluffs
Along the bay and hear the sounds of the potential crabs
Scratching in their caves. From already having seen,
We could believe in the hard pull of the new children's
Children's children up that beach.

And what if the speck of a grunion egg just beginning
Should be planted inside the embryo heart of our next child born?
Then wouldn't he know from the start how he was to rise
Like silver fruit in a swollen tide, how he was to start up
And break through elements? Wouldn't he know in his lungs,
Before it happened, the sudden changing dimension
Of his own breath? Wouldn't he understand how he was bound
To decide to head straight for what he already knew was coming,
And couldn't he tell us everything we need to know
About convictions like that?

Lineage

Before the day when Kioka was converted,
Proclaiming himself a born Indian, he knew nothing
About coupsticks or calumets or pinto ponies
Or his own bare legs below breechcloths or famine
On a prairie in dry, waist-high grasses or nightmares
Behind eyes frozen shut with sleet. Before that day,
He had never seen or touched the angel of the abyss
Or the enemy of the abyss.

It was only after Kioka became a perfect Indian
That his elderly mother grew gradually obsessed
With clay pottery and reeds, appearing on summer days
In her lace peignoir at dawn, gathering mud
In hand-woven baskets by the river bottom. It was then
That his sister amazed everyone by creating,
On the croquet courts, a multicolored sand painting
Of sun gods and fire gods by heart.

And after Kioka had been a perfect Indian
For fifty moons, his father's physician found
Strains of red corpuscles from Fleet Deer, Warrior Girl
And Cocotyl in samples of the family's blood.
And, in an old painted gourd filled with raw chocolate
And hammered silver jewelry, his uncle discovered
A portrait, never seen before, of his great-paternal-aunt
Dressed in green quetzal feathers with her hair dyed blue.

Now Kioka's brother can call wolves or wild turkeys
With a weird tremolo, and they come. His first cousin
Can perform ritual music on shell trumpet, clay whistle
Or two-toned drums. And the relative who ridiculed Kioka,
Making gestures behind his back, was visited twice
By night stranglers smelling of bear grease and piñon nuts.
Afterward, when he could speak again, he gave
Seven sincere prayers for the spirits of Serpent Woman
And Rain-God-with-Jaguar-Teeth.

Kioka, having no permanent abode and having reinterpreted
His sense of direction, rarely sees his family
And will not attest personally to these phenomena.
But the oldest white-winged hawk in the canyon, circling
The sacred place where the graves of Kioka's ancestors
Have now come to be, cries the names of his six fathers
Day after day into the rock-walled sky.
And everyone who hears it knows it to be so.

Intermediary

For John A. and Arthur

This is what I ask: that if they must be taken
They be taken like the threads of the cotton grass
Are taken by the summer wind, excited and dizzy
And safe, flying inside their own seeds;
And if they must be lost that they be lost
Like leaves of the water starwort
Are lost, submerged and rising over and over
In the slow-rooted current by the bank.

I ask that they always be found
With the same sure and easy touch
The early morning stillness uses to find itself
In needles of dew on each hyssop in the ditch.

And may they see everything the boatman bug,
Shining inside its bubble of air, sees
Through silver skin in the pond-bottom mud,
And may they be obliged in the same way the orb snail,
Sucking on sedges in shallow water, is obliged.
And may they be promised everything a single blade
Of sweet flag, kept by the grip of the elmid
On its stem, kept by the surrounding call
Of the cinnamon teal, kept by its line
In the marsh-filled sky, is promised.

Outloud, in public and in writing, I ask again
That solace come to them like sun comes
To the egg of the longspur, penetrating the shell,
Settling warmth inside the potential heart
And beginnings of bone. And I ask that they remember
Their grace in the same way the fetal bird remembers light
Inside the blackness of its gathering skull inside
The cave of its egg.

And with the same attention a streamer of ice
Moving with the moon commands, with the same decision
The grassland plovers declare as they rise
From the hayfields into the evening sky,
I ask that these pleas of mine arrest the notice
Of all those angels already possessing a lasting love
For fine and dauntless boys like mine.

If a Son Asks

Luke 11:11

I would bring him hatchetfish, goatfish
And albacore. I would bring shad with the finest
Silver-sloughing scales, the gristled stems
Of broad-nosed cat, fat orange salmon filled
With eggs and slick sturgeon round with oily roe,
The rich milt of mackerel, tarpon still turning,
Their grey gills revealing the inner movements
Of the prairie rose, and the intent of the sea caught
In the clear salty syrup of the yellow-fin's eye,
And each transparent scale of the carp showing
Its circling rings as a still lake shows time
By a single drop of rain.

If a son asks, I would bring
The invisible fish in the treetops and the way
It uses sunlight for water and the way it shapes
The air between branches and the way it holds itself
Against the rushing current of the wind.

And if he asks, the fish keeping the bracing structure
Of cobwebs in its bones, the fanning of bracken
Fronds in its veins, keeping the sliding sky of summer
For a pale blue flank, the black tail-ripple of night
In its quick forward swerve; the fish stroking
In darkness behind the eyes, if he asks, treading
Like sleep, the one that can take fathers and swallow

Mothers and consume sons, making a world of its belly
As it sounds, sounding deep, the backwash of space
Roaring and cresting over its rolling descent, I would give
That fish in its entirety to a son who asks
And kiss him as he takes it and hold him,
And hold him while he eats.

The Birth Song and the Death Song

One of them moves like a continuum of stars rising
Out of the lake on the east, making, by its crossing,
A void to cross above poplar and chain fern,
Night-threading teal and a nebula of carp.
And one of them moves like a season of stars
Sinking into the reeds and water lilies
Of the lake on the west, making, by its passing,
An interval to pass far below mud-laden roots
Of arum, the bright undersides of wheel snails,
Hydra and yellow-budded lotus.

One turns itself inside out, exposing
Its tender intimacies to every rush
And hook and spire of mayhem and mercy.
And the other one gathers into itself continually,
Surrounding every spicule and template
Of pity and quickening and atrocity
With its most private solicitudes.

And the first one releases suddenly
Like a spider dropping and swinging free
In the evening light between branchtop and earth.
And the last one accepts release instantaneously
Like a moment of evening light becoming
The floating liberty of a spider's fall
Between branchtop and earth.

The finer one is the opening deep
In the flower of the purple pleatleaf leading
From the disorder of eternity to an upright
Petal of blue cobwebbed in morning sun.
And the greater one is the tight
Closing of a single seed of pleatleaf
Fastening around the certain infinity
Of its only place in the field.

And one is like strong wooden arms spread wide
And sailing, and the other is like the steady
Bracing bones of a rising kite, by which means
Both *do* support and endure at once
The soaring tension of the paper soul
As it spirals and spins—sunside,
Earthside—across the open spaces of the sky.

III

Little Fugue

Felicia and Albert, running through the thin grasses
In the mown field this afternoon, are attempting
To keep up with the red-tailed hawk's shadow
As it glides across the pond and the meadow.

Cecil can also see the red-tailed hawk
In the sky in the pond as he dangles his feet
In the water, his toes startling the basking killifish.

The curious killifish rise slowly now to suck
At Cecil's toes in the same way the hawk soars upward
Toward the basking sun, its winged shadow becoming a small
Black fish swimming through the slender grasses.

Cecil sees the killifish as flashing slips of light
Darting through the feathers of the hawk as it glides
Across the blue water of the heavens at his feet.

Albert thinks Felicia's laughter soaring
Over the meadow is like slips of light
Flashing off the fins of little killifish.

Felicia can imagine slips of sun darting like killifish
In the sky between her legs as she runs after the wings
Of the red-tailed hawk over the mown meadow.

Cecil can see the red-tailed hawk growing smaller
And smaller, circling his feet, disappearing finally
Into the black mouth of a single killifish gliding
At the bottom of the pond.

The killifish, simultaneously swallowed like a slip of sun
By the shadow of the hawk, can be seen as itself once again
Inside Felicia's laughter.

Felicia, catching up and stepping on the shadow
Of the hawk, has finally seen the black wings of her feet.

When Sonia calls from the porch, telling everyone
That the magician has arrived for the party, all the sounds
Of finned light passing like laughter over the stubbled sun
Are swallowed by Albert's announcement
That this is the end of the game.

Parlor Game on a Snowy Winter Night

Albert, standing at the window, began by saying,
"False china eggs in a chicken's nest stimulate
The hen to lay eggs that are real,
And they also occasionally fool weasels."

"Telling the truth to a chicken then,"
Replied Sonia, "must be considered a grievous sin,
And deception, in this case, an extraordinary virtue."

"Chickens, brooding on china eggs as well as real ones,"
Said Cecil, rubbing his chin, "might regard glass eggs
As admirably false, but a weasel nosing the nest
Would consider glass eggs a malevolent tomfoolery
And the devil's own droppings."

"A weasel, testing the reality of eggs,
Must find glass and albumen
Equally easy to identify," continued Albert.

"China eggs, whether warm or not," said Felicia,
Mocking herself in the mirror, "at least consistently maintain
Their existence as false eggs."

"Perhaps the true egg, unable to maintain its reality
For long, is actually a weak imitation
Of the eternal nature of the glass egg," said Albert,
Drawing his initials on the frosty windowpane.

"Someone must investigate how the real image
Of a false egg in the chicken's true eye causes the cells
Of a potential egg to become an actuality," said Gordon,
Laying his book on the table.

"Can we agree then that the false china egg,
A deceptive but actual instigator,
Is the first true beginning of the chicken yard?"
Asked Sonia, filling in the last line of the game sheet.

Albert, rushing outdoors to discover
What the dogs had cornered in the brush beside the barn,
Found a weasel in the snow
With bloody yolk on its whiskers and a broken tooth.

Observing the Questions of a Grey Sky

What we observe is not nature itself but nature
exposed to our method of questioning.
                    —*Werner Heisenberg*

Who would suppose that one sky by itself
Could contain so many colors called grey—
Blue grey, beige grey, toad grey, and broken grey,
Birch grey, severe grey, and barely perceived,
Sable grey at mid-heart, and never perceived but postulated,
The lavender grey of flowers found in winter moss
Beneath juniper trees? To the north a lateral column
Of soldier grey rises like smoke, forced without wind
To its own statuesque devices. Low in the south
An illusion of grey covers the sun.

And the sky above possesses the same multiple greys
As the sky in the lake below. Which sky is it then
That moves backward through the flight of five black birds
Skimming the tundra grey surfaces? And which sky holds
The five black shadows with wings in its clouds?
If the birds should soar, in which direction
Would they fall? If the birds should dive,
Into which clouds would they disappear?

Does the grey body of the wooden shed beside the lake
Find an aspect of itself in the slivered grey
Of the eleventh layer of cloud above? Does the loon
Learn something new of its breast matched perfectly
In color with the knife grey edge of the sky

Against which it perches? Does the meadow vole
Become forever related to cumulus vapor
By being its identical brother in grey this afternoon?
What if the brown grey grasses of the field
Are simply the limited vision of the sky making seeds?

Where is the grey parting of the sky
Made by the bow of the boat moving across the lake?
And in this wide expanse, who can find the grey shoulder
Of father's coat or the grey separation of your footsteps
On the path or the grey ring of the rock thrown in anger
Into the sky? Must the entire history of grey descend
Forever beyond the bottom of the lake or can it disappear
Diagonally into the dark line of the circular horizon?
Remember how the motion of grey can come suddenly like rain
Breaking the sky into overlapping circles in the lake below.

Any question occasioned by the grey sky this evening
Must be part of the sky and a metallic grey itself,
Easily observed in the mirror of grey
Found in a reflective eye.

Finding the Tattooed Lady in the Garden

Circus runaway, tattooed from head to toe in yellow
Petals and grape buds, rigid bark and dust-streaked
Patterns of summer, she lives naked among the hedges
And bordered paths of the garden. She hardly
Has boundaries there, so definite is her place.

Sometimes the golden flesh of the butterfly,
Quiet and needled in the spot of sun on her shoulder,
Can be seen and sometimes the wide blue wing
Of her raised hand before the maple and sometimes
The crisscrossed thicket, honeysuckle and fireweed,
Of her face. As she poses perfectly, her legs apart,
Some people can find the gentian-smooth meadow-skin showing
Through the distant hickory groves painted up her thighs
And the warm white windows of open sky appearing
Among the rose blossoms and vines of her breasts.

Shadow upon tattooed shadow upon real shadow,
She is there in the petaled skin of the iris
And the actual violet scents overlapping
At the bend of her arm, beneath and beyond
The initial act announcing the stems
Of the afternoon leaved and spread
In spires of green along her ribs, the bronze
Lizard basking at her navel.

Some call her searched-for presence the being
Of being, the essential garden of the garden.
And some call the continuing postulation
Of her location the only underlying structure,
The single form of flux, the final proof
And presence of crafted synonymy.
And whether the shadows of the sweetgum branches
Above her shift in the breeze across her breasts
Or whether she herself sways slightly
Beneath the still star-shaped leaves of the quiet
Forest overhead or whether the sweetgum shadows
Tattooed on her torso swell and linger
As the branches above are stirred by her breath,
The images possessed by the seekers are one
And the same when they know them as such.

And in the dark of late evening,
Isn't it beautiful the way they watch for her
To turn slowly, displaying the constellations
Penned in light among the black leaves
And blossoms of her back, the North Star
In its only coordinates shining at the base
Of her neck, the way they study the first glowing
Rim of the moon rising by its own shape
From the silvered curve of her brilliant hip?

The Compassion of the Iris

Compassion, if it could be seen, might look
Like an early blossom of iris,
Something like an uplands flower on a wooded
Morning, five purple suns visible on its petals
As five points of a shallow dawn.

If compassion appeared as an iris
It would be possible to trace the actual outline
Of its arched and crested edges, to describe
The crucial motivation coming at the juncture
Of its yellow-ridged sepals, to examine
The significance in the structure of white veins
Covering its calyx, to discover, by touch,
The hidden meat of the bulb from which the origin
Of its concept must first have arisen.

And maybe the benevolence inherent to ordinary
Purple-streaked flowers could be understood
As they cover, without intrusion, the lowest rim
Of evening, when they draw their violet lines
As carefully as dusk draws time above the dusty floor
Of the pine barrens. Corms and stems,
Lobes and basal clusters might be
Recognized as the subtlest, most crucial
Tenderness of the soil.

And it might be possible to imagine how the bond
Creating the central fact of compassion is exactly
The same fact binding a gene of violet
In the ovary of the iris, how compassion
Possesses the same grip on its own form
As the perfumed rhizome maintains
On the tight molecule of its scent.

And what astonishing union is it that takes place
On the day when compassion is offered as a gift
In the form of spring iris gathered from the field?

One might wonder if the iris
Should be studied meticulously in order to reveal
The intricacies of compassion,
Or whether one should act compassionately
In order to fully perceive the peculiarities
Of that extraordinary blue-violet flower.

Reaching the Audience

From the introduction to *The First Book of Iridaceae*

We will start with a single blue dwarf iris
Appearing as a purple dot on a hairstreak
Butterfly seen in a distant pine barrens and proceed
Until we end with a single point of purple spiraling
Like an invisible wing in the center of the flower
Making fact.

We will investigate a stand of blue flags crimsoned
By the last sun still showing over the smoky edges
Of the ravine and illustrate in sequence the glazing
Of those iris by the wet gold of an early dawn.

We will survey a five-mile field of purple iris
Holding bristle-legged insects under the tips
Of their stamens and measure the violet essence
Gathered at the bases of their wings and devote
One section to a molecule of iris fragrance
Preserved and corked in a slender glass.

There will be a composition replicating the motion
Of the iris rolling sun continually over its rills
And another for the stillness of the iris sucking ivory
Moonlight through its hollows making ivory roots.

There will be photographs in series of the eyes
Of a woman studying the sepals of an iris
In a lavender vase and a seven-page account of the crested
Iris burning at midnight in the shape of its flame
And six oriental paintings of purple petals torn apart
And scattered over snow beneath birches and a poem
Tracing a bouquet of blue iris tied together like balloons
Floating across the highest arc of a spring heaven.

There will be an analysis of the word of the iris
In the breath of the dumb and an investigation
Of the touch of the iris in the fingertips of the blind
And a description of the iris-shaped spaces existing
In the forest before the forest became itself
And a delineation of those same blade-thin spaces
Still existing after the forest has been lost again.

It is the sole purpose of these volumes-in-progress
To ensure that anyone stopped anywhere in any perspective
Or anyone caught forever in any crease of time or anyone
Left inside the locked and folded bud of any dream
Will be able to recognize something on these pages
And remember.

Discovering Your Subject

Painting a picture of the same shrimp boat
Every day of your life might not be so boring.
For a while you could paint only in the mornings,
Each one different, the boat gold in the new sun
On your left, or the boat in predawn fog condensing
Mist. You might have to wait years, rising early
Over and over, to catch that one winter morning when frost
Becomes a boat. You could attempt to capture
The fragile potential inherent in that event.

You might want to depict the easy half-circle
Movements of the boat's shadows crossing over themselves
Through the day. You could examine every line
At every moment—the tangle of nets caught
In the orange turning of evening, the drape of the ropes
Over the rising moon.

You could spend considerable time just concentrating
On boat and birds—Boat with Birds Perched on Bow,
Boat with Birds Overhead, Shadows of Birds Covering
Hull and Deck, or Boat the Size of a Bird,
Bird in the Heart of the Boat, Boat with Wings,
Boat in Flight. Any endeavor pursued long enough
Assumes a momentum and direction all its own.

Or you might decide to lie down one day behind a clump
Of marsh rosemary on the beach, to see the boat embedded
In the blades of the saltwort or show how strangely
The stalk of the clotbur can rise higher than the mast.
Boat Caught like a Flower in the Crotch of the Sand Verbena.

After picturing the boat among stars, after discovering
The boat as revealed by rain, you might try painting
The boat in the eye of the gull or the boat in the eye
Of the sun or the boat in the eye of a storm
Or the eye trapped in the window of the boat.
You could begin a series of self-portraits—The Boat
In the Eye of the Remorseful Painter, The Boat in the Eye
Of the Blissful Painter, The Boat in the Eye of the Blind Painter,
The Boat in the Lazy Painter Forgetting His Eye.

Finally one day when the boat's lines are drawn in completely,
It will begin to move away, gradually changing its size,
Enlarging the ocean, requiring less sky, and suddenly it might seem
That you are the one moving. You are the one altering space,
Gliding easily over rough surfaces toward the mark
Between the ocean and the sky. You might see clearly,
For the first time, the boat inside the painter inside the boat
Inside the eye watching the painter moving beyond himself.
You must remember for us the exact color and design of that.

"The Tree Has Captured My Soul"

For van Gogh

When they found him mad in the field
On his knees, gripping the hard wooden trunk
Of his own living soul, it could never be said
How it happened, whether the soul of the tree,
Its branches rising and interlocking like bones,
Had disguised itself as skeleton and penetrated
The vision of his body that way undetected;
Or whether his soul willingly turned the vision of itself
Inside its own socket and became the pure white tree
Of its own interlocking; or whether he saw and testified
To the fragmentary parting of his soul caught
Among the wind and branches spreading across his canvas;
Or whether he captured his own body in the turning
Brushstrokes of a thousand yellow leaves and forfeited thereby
The treeless autonomy of his soul here on earth;
Or whether he lost the whole tree of his eye but gained
A vision of the veins of his soul rising and branching
Toward light; or whether the wind turned the soul
Of each yellow leaf inside its own socket
Until his eye was united everlastingly with that movement;
Or whether he saw the shimmering perception
Of that tree lift his body, light as a soul,
On the tips of its branches forever toward heaven.

But it is known that he came fully awake among them
In the field, his arms around his body
As if it were rooted in the earth, seeing
The illuminating wind of his soul for the first time
In all the possible movements of yellow
Each visionary leaf could offer him.

First Notes from One Born and Living
in an Abandoned Barn

Every dusty bar and narrow streak of brilliance
Originating from white slits and roof crevices
Or streaming to the floor all day in one solid column
From the opening directly overhead
Are only light.

The rising tatter of weed ticks under the door
And the quick unseen banging of shingles above
Are named the sudden and the unexpected.

Silence is understood to be the straw-flecked
Morasses of webs consistently filling the corners
With a still grey filagree of dirt, and meditation
Is called orb weaver and funnel spider tugging
At their ropes, working and stitching
With the synchronization of their flexible nails.

The farthest limits to which the eyes can see—
The rotten board walls and the high wind-stopped
Eaves—are the boundaries the mind clearly recognizes
As the farthest edges of itself, and the steel-blue forks
Of the swallows bumping and tapping along the ledges
Of the rafters all afternoon define again
The barriers of the acknowledged. Realization
Is simply the traceable expansion gradually filling
All the spaces known as barn.

And at night the point at which the slow downward swoop
Of the bat first begins its new angle upward is called
Proof of the power of the body's boundaries.
And what it is believed the snake experiences as it slides
The line of its belly along the thigh
Is thigh. The length of the arm is nothing more
Than the length the mouse crawls before its feet
Are felt no more. And what it is imagined the owl sees
As it stares from the eaves directly into the eyes
Of the one it perceives is called identity.

What appears in the opening of the roof at night
Is only what the barn envelopes and holds.
What the mind envelopes and holds in the opening
Of the roof is called the beyond.
And the beyond is either the definition of disappearance
Discovered by the bats, or else it is the rectangular
Body of stars defining the place of the roof, or else
It is the black opening looking down on the starlit
Rectangle creating the eyes, or else it is the entire
Inner surface of the face composed of stars, or else
It is the first lucky guess of the mind at the boundless
Which is exactly what has caused the need to begin tonight
The documented expansion inherent to these notes.

The Form of the Message

Through the spring afternoon the spangled
Fritillary and the red admiral spread
The only information available concerning floating
Orange and scarlet furls of open sky.
The bullfrog is an obvious messenger bringing
Web-toed proclamations of sloughs
And ditches, announcing details of drift
In the easy hang of its white-legged body in the pond.
And the map turtle is the angel of itself
Declaring red-eyed visions of delicacy in slug
Of snail and clam. And snail and clam embody notices
Of suck and draw, the facts of hard-shelled
Slips of living mud.

The quiet in the budded hook
Of the mossy plumatella delivers the still, perfect
Angel of its own silence, and the prayer of the fanning
Bluegill is the form of its breathing message.
The angel of the primrose willow
Is the swaying leaf of its own graceful prayer.
Whistling and scaling just above the tips of the reeds,
The message of the meadowlark creates the shape
Of its reception in the ear. The pattern of muscle
And breath and ripple in the lark's trilling throat
Is the form of the angel it has always been.
The message that the ear proclaims is the act
Of reception it performs.

Father, this prayer of messengers
I bring to you this afternoon
Is its own message, an angel of good news
In the form of the spring field.
Listen now, for me, to the shape of your ear.

The Tongues of Angels

I Cor. 13:1

The split-second slivers of spiny lizard, sheep frog,
Bufo and chirping marnocki, the stunted ivory knobs
Of tortoise and carp, word from the facile thread
Of the arrow crab, from the yellow tongues of honey
Mesquite, from the red sentence buried in the beak
Of the wheatear, from the mouths of carpenter ants
Perceiving the honeydew language of sucking bugs;

By the coiled power of moth and swallowtail,
The green speech of grass on the tongues of nanny
And sheep, the multilingual form of purple in layered
Larkspur and bloom of chickory, by the quiet syntax
Of the afternoon rising in the air above stubbled
Meadows, the rock tongue of evening mute along the strata
Of the canyon's edge, by the tongues of the sun
Speaking through curtains of blowing lace,

Let me speak, let me learn to speak with love
By the tongues of these loved angels, father, tonight,
To ease, for a moment, the sound of the stuttering cymbal,
My own persistent babble of brass.

Being Accomplished

Balancing on her haunches, the mouse can accomplish
Certain things with her hands. She can pull the hull
From a barley seed in paperlike pieces the size of threads.
She can turn and turn a crumb to create smaller motes
The size of her mouth. She can burrow in sand and grasp
One single crystal grain in both of her hands.
A quarter of a dried pea can fill her palm.

She can hold the earless, eyeless head
Of her furless baby and push it to her teat.
The hollow of its mouth must feel like the invisible
Confluence sucking continually deep inside a pink flower.

And the mouse is almost compelled
To see everything. Her hand, held up against the night sky,
Can scarcely hide Venus or Polaris
Or even a corner of the crescent moon.
It can cover only a fraction of the blue moth's wing.
Its shadow could never mar or blot enough of the evening
To matter.

Imagine the mouse with her spider-sized hands
Holding to a branch of dead hawthorn in the middle
Of the winter field tonight. Picture the night pressing in
Around those hands, forced, simply by their presence,

To fit its great black bulk exactly around every hair
And every pinlike nail, forced to outline perfectly
Every needle-thin bone without crushing one, to carry
Its immensity right up to the precise boundary of flesh
But no farther. Think how the heavy weight of infinity,
Expanding outward in all directions forever, is forced,
Nevertheless, to mold itself right here and now
To every peculiarity of those appendages.

And even the mind, capable of engulfing
The night sky, capable of enclosing infinity,
Capable of surrounding itself inside any contemplation,
Has been obliged, for this moment, to accommodate the least
Grasp of that mouse, the dot of her knuckle, the accomplishment
Of her slightest intent.

Inside God's Eye

As if his eye had no boundaries, at night
All the heavens are visible there. The stars drift
And hesitate inside that sphere like white seeds
Sinking in a still, dark lake. Spirals of brilliance,
They float silently and slowly deeper and deeper
Into the possible expansion of his acuity.
And within that watching, illumination like the moon
Is uncovered petal by petal as a passing cloud clears
The open white flowers of the shining summer plum.

Inside god's eye, light spreads as afternoon spreads,
Accepting the complications of water burr and chestnut,
The efforts of digger bee and cuckoo bee. Even the barest
Light gathers and concentrates there like a ray
Of morning reaching the thinnest nerve of a fairy shrimp
At the center of a pond. And like evening, light
Bends inside the walls of god's eye to make
Skywide globes of fuchsia and orange, violet-tipped
Branches and violet-tinged wings set against a red dusk.

Lines from the tangle of dodder, bindweed
And honeysuckle, from the interweaving knot
Of seaweed and cones, patterns from the network
Of blowing shadow and flashing poplar, fill
And define the inner surface moment of his retina.

And we, we are the only point of reversal
Inside his eye, the only point of light
That turns back on itself and by that turning
Saves time from infinity and saves motion
From obscurity. We are the vessel and the blood
And the pulse he sees as he sees the eye watching
The vision inside his eye in the perfect mirror
Held constantly before his face.

About the Author

Pattiann Rogers has received several prizes for her poetry. Her first book, *The Expectations of Light,* won the Voertman Poetry Award from the Texas Institute of Letters in 1982. She received two awards from *Poetry* magazine, the Eunice Tietjens and Bess Hokin awards, and two from *Poetry Northwest,* the Young Poets and Theodore Roethke prizes. She has also received an NEA grant and a Guggenheim fellowship. Rogers is a graduate of the University of Missouri at Columbia (B.A. 1961) and the University of Houston (M.A. 1981). She lives in Stafford, Texas.

About the Book

This book was typeset by G&S Typesetters of Austin, Texas, in Bembo with Bembo bold display type, was printed on 60 pound Miami Book Vellum paper by Kingsport Press of Kingsport, Tennessee, and was bound by Kingsport Press. The design is by Joyce Kachergis Book Design and Production of Bynum, North Carolina.

Wesleyan University Press.